GREAT MYSTERIES
The Loch Ness Monster
OPPOSING VIEWPOINTS®

Look for these and other exciting *Great Mysteries: Opposing Viewpoints* books:

GREAT MYSTERIES
The Loch Ness Monster
OPPOSING VIEWPOINTS®

by Robert San Souci

Greenhaven Press, Inc.   P.O. Box 289009, San Diego, California 92198-0009

Library of Congress Cataloging-in-Publication Data

San Souci, Robert D.
    The Loch Ness Monster

    (Great mysteries: opposing viewpoints)
    Bibliography: p.
    Includes index
    Summary: Explores the mystery of the legendary beast said to inhabit Scotland's Loch Ness and which has always eluded scientific scrutiny. Is it a leftover dinosaur or a harmless folktale?
        1. Loch Ness Monster—Juvenile literature. [1. Loch Ness monster. 2. Monsters] I. Title. II. Series: Great mysteries (Saint Paul, Minn.)
    QL89.2.L6S23   1989   001.9'44   89-12026
    ISBN 0-89908-072-3

© Copyright 1989 by Greenhaven Press, Inc.
Produced by Carnival Enterprises, Minneapolis, MN
Every effort has been made to trace owners of copyright material.

For my nieces:
Andrea, Yvette, Noelle, and Shelley;
and nephews:
Justin, Mark, Nick, and Robert.
Wishing each a little "Nessie"—
a sense of wonder and adventure—
to last a lifetime.

Contents

Introduction

This book is written for the curious—those who want to explore the mysteries that are everywhere. To be human is to be constantly surrounded by wonderment. How do birds fly? Are ghosts real? Can animals and people communicate? Was King Arthur a real person or a myth? Why did Amelia Earhart disappear? Did history really happen the way we think it did? Where did the world come from? Where is it going?

Great Mysteries: Opposing Viewpoints books are intended to offer the reader an opportunity to explore some of the many mysteries that both trouble and intrigue us. For the span of each book, we want the reader to feel that he or she is a scientist investigating the extinction of the dinosaurs, an archaeologist searching for clues to the origin of the great Egyptian pyramids, a psychic detective testing the existence of ESP.

One thing all mysteries have in common is that there is no ready answer. Often there are *many* answers but none on which even the majority of authorities agrees. *Great Mysteries: Opposing Viewpoints* books introduce the intriguing views of the experts, allowing the reader to participate in their explorations, their theories, and their disagreements as they try to explain the mysteries of our world.

But most readers won't want to stop here. These *Great Mysteries: Opposing Viewpoints* aim to stimulate the reader's curiosity. Although truth is often impossible to discover, the search is fascinating. It is up to the reader to examine the evidence, to decide whether the answer is there—or to explore further.

"Penetrating so many secrets, we cease to believe in the unknowable. But there it sits nevertheless, calmly licking its chops."

H.L. Mencken, American essayist

Prologue

The Riddle of Loch Ness

On November 13, 1972, four Scottish teenagers walking home from school passed by Borlum Bay and got quite a surprise. It was one of those pretty, sunny afternoons permitting a clear view across Lake (Loch) Ness. Suddenly they spotted what they described as a thirty-five foot monster. The "thing" moved something like a "caterpillar" just under the surface, was "wet and shiny," and had dark gray skin. From time to time, the boys said, parts of its body rose several feet above the water, leaving ripples as it swam. The terrified youngsters did not see a head or neck, or were too startled to take a really careful look. And the encounter was over quickly. In just two minutes, they reported, the mystery creature dove underwater and did not come up again. At least not while they watched that afternoon.

Running home, the boys told everybody who would listen about the creature they had seen at the southern end of Loch Ness. Some people believed them; most scoffed. But the sighting was just one more piece of the best-known and most argued about unsolved mysteries of the twentieth century. Is there a monster, perhaps a dinosaur out of the past, living

The most famous photograph of the Loch Ness monster was taken on April 19, 1934 by R.K. Wilson, a surgeon from London. It is often called "The Surgeon's Photograph."

> "This monster does exist."
>
> Professor Colin Magregor, quoted in *Sea Monsters*

> "The fact that almost all the monster sightings are very brief—a few minutes or less—is also consistent with mirage effects."
>
> Henry Bauer, *The Enigma of Loch Ness*

in the 925-foot depths of the lake? Might there even be more than one? No one knows.

Many eyewitnesses claim to have seen "Nessie," as the creature has come to be called, swimming. A few reported seeing it on land near the shores of Loch Ness. Believers point to the number of photographs taken over the years as proof that the Loch Ness mystery creature exists.

But just as many people claim that witnesses were mistaken, or made up stories for their own reasons. They point to the lack of bones or bodies. The photographs, they say, are either unclear or can be explained away or are outright fakes.

So believers continue to believe, others treat the matter as nothing more than a fantastic story, and a small group of scientists persist in trying to find out the truth using increasingly sophisticated underwater investigation equipment.

Loch Ness is located in northern Scotland near the city of Inverness.

Urquhart Bay, noted for its ancient castle, is one of the deepest places in the Loch.

One

Why Is Loch Ness a Good Hiding Place?

Loch Ness is twenty-four miles long and two miles wide. To someone standing on either end, it seems to stretch as far as the eye can see. On either side of the dark, inky water are steep tree-covered mountains rising to heights of almost three thousand feet.

It is a solitary region, located in the heart of the Scottish Highlands. Few towns have been built nearby because the weather becomes very cold near the lake in winter. However, the city of Inverness is located at its northern end. On the southern side, a few fishing villages and resort hotels are tucked away along the shore. The town of Fort Augustus lies at the southern tip. Breaking the sparseness, the ruins of an ancient castle stand lonely guard at Urquhart Bay on the west side of the loch.

The loch is the largest body of fresh water in Great Britain. It was carved out by a glacier, a sheet of ice perhaps 4,000 feet thick, about ten thousand years ago. But the area around it is older than that—much older. The Great Glen in which Loch Ness rests is believed to be at least 300 million years old.

At one time the entire Highland area was covered with ice. Before and after the Ice Age, Loch Ness

The cold, dark and deep waters of Loch Ness have added to the mystery surrounding the creature.

was part of the North Sea and filled with saltwater. In time, the land began to rise, and Loch Ness was cut off from the sea except for the five-mile-long River Ness which flows out of the loch at its northern end. Some believers have held that it is possible that some prehistoric beast got caught in the loch before it was closed off from the sea. There might even have been a herd of them, some argue, to allow for generations of Nessies. Over the years, they say, as the loch turned from salt to fresh water, such creatures might have gradually adapted to the change. There is scientific evidence that other creatures have evolved in just this way.

The Murky Loch

The saltwater disappeared because five rivers and forty-five mountain streams pour fresh water into the lake. But it is not clear water. Instead the water is stained dark brown by particles of peat seeping from the local bogs. "The problem is," one scuba diver wrote, "the waters of Loch Ness are black. Millions of tiny pieces of soft coal are constantly being washed into the lake. They make it impossible to see below the surface. Underwater photography is out of the question." Peat is mostly moss which has changed to carbon through natural processes. The peat which floats in the loch not only colors its water, it makes it impossible to see through it. Peering into Loch Ness, visitors do not see the bottom, they see only a few feet below the murky surface. Low-flying helicopters or planes on search missions also cannot see anything clearly. Boats have even less luck. Divers entering the lake have described their experiences in the gloom as "frightening." Author Gerald Snyder writes, "In turbid water, such as Loch Ness, visibility can be limited to a few feet at most. And because water has a filtering effect, blocking out light, the deeper you swim, the darker it gets. Blue tapers into gray, gray becomes

black, and at some depths visibility may be limited to a few inches."

The surface merely hints at what lies below. Loch Ness is 925 feet deep in areas near Urquhart Bay. There may be areas that are deeper still. That is a lot of space in which a creature, or many creatures, might hide.

Nor does a beast have to worry about its home freezing over. Twice as deep as the North Sea, Loch Ness never freezes. However it is not warm either. The bottom temperature is an average forty-two degrees Fahrenheit, while the surface is a mere fifty-eight degrees. If a creature enjoyed cool water, Loch Ness's environment would be ideal.

The cold, slightly acid water of the loch also could hide the death of any monster living in it. In a warm lake, a dead body will fill with gas and rise to

Is this the trail of Nessie moving just beneath the surface? This wake was captured on film taken by Malcolm Irvine, December 12, 1933.

American electronics engineers Alan Kielar and Rikki Razdan examine a dart gun used for tagging underwater animals.

the surface. The gas is formed by bacteria feeding on the body and causing the carcass to rot. But the peat in the loch causes an acidic condition, and in very cold acid water, bacteria slow down. Instead of building up, gas escapes, and the animal's body sinks to the bottom instead of rising to the surface. Many monster remains could lie hidden at the muddy bottom of this deep lake, and nobody would know.

Adding to the lake's ability to camouflage its inhabitants are the small earthquakes which occur every few years. Geologists say the lake is located on a fault line, a huge crack going deep into the earth's surface. Divers report these tremors have created large underwater cracks which could also provide hiding places.

The loch has places near its bottom where the

sides form overhangs. Beneath these ledges almost any size creature could hide safely, perhaps detectable only by the most precise modern equipment aimed at exactly the right spot.

For many years rumors have persisted that there are deep caves, caverns, valleys and secret passages to the North Sea in the lake. So far, the existence of these has neither been proven or disproven. "If there are such caverns," author Gerald Snyder writes, "and if they slope upwards, it would be possible for large portions to reach inland, above the level of the water. This would give the monsters, if, for instance, they are mammals, all the air they would need and keep them well hidden from human eyes, which could explain the relatively rare sightings."

Though the surrounding mountains are covered

Kielar and Razdan designed and built this sonar tracking grid to penetrate the murky depths of the loch and "see" Nessie.

with trees and shrubs, around the lake itself few plants can be seen. But there are plenty of fish: big brown trout, salmon weighing thirty pounds or more, pike, char, sticklebacks, and masses of eels. While there would be slim pickings for a huge plant-eating beast, a creature that ate fish would find sufficient food in the lake.

There is yet another thing that makes Loch Ness an ideal hiding place for a large water dwelling beast. Even if Nessie should come to the surface occasionally, it might not be easily seen here either. The blackish-brown waters of Loch Ness, when quiet, act almost like a mirror. They reflect shapes from clouds and flying birds. A darkish head, hump or fin might just seem another reflection.

The prospect of seeing the fabled monster draws thousands every year to Loch Ness.

Anyone who attempts to "monster hunt" for any length of time discovers Loch Ness has its violent moods. If a wind springs up, eight-foot-high waves soon follow in its wake along the loch's entire length. Moreover, the steep walls on either side of the lake make it into a wind tunnel, stiffening the waves and making them even more powerful. There are days, observers note, when the wind churns the surface so much that it is impossible to see a smooth spot anywhere. Anyone braving the freezing wind might think he or she sees a head or hump, though it would only be a shadow made by a wave. On the other hand, Nessie might swim quite freely during a windstorm and nobody could see it. The waves would screen the creature completely.

Nessie Weather

Another type of possible camouflage occurs on calm sunny days—the type of days when people are most likely to claim they have seen Nessie. Weather reports of "clear, flat, calm, sunny," are often accompanied by a hazy mist covering the lake, causing a strange type of distortion to take place in the air. A flock of birds, a log, a floating barrel may take on weird shapes. These shapes may also appear larger than they really are. It is called "Nessie weather" by the locals accustomed to Loch Ness's visual tricks.

"At Loch Ness," author Henry Bauer writes, "the opportunities to be deceived are legion. When the water is relatively smooth and the wind gusty but not too strong, the wind-ruffled surface has a silvery appearance and calm patches stand out as black 'humps' of varying sizes and shapes." On a calm day, when there are only small wavelets, Bauer continues, "their tops frequently look like rounded or angular black bodies knifing through the water, coming up and diving again."

Boats may also contribute to the false sightings. Roy P. Mackal, in his *Monsters of Loch Ness*, com-

"All do agree on one point: Nessie moves fast. Further, most believe that the monster is very shy. Once it is spotted, it dives out of sight."

James B. Sweeney, *Sea Monsters*

"There is no scientific evidence whatsoever of monsters in Loch Ness, but a handful of individuals will go on seeing them there."

Author Ronald Binns, quoted in *The Wall Street Journal*

The long, narrow shape of Loch Ness produces many striking wave patterns that skeptics claim are the real source of Nessie sightings.

ments, "Because of the long and narrow shape of the lake, long spectacular trains of waves resembling black humps are produced, often up to one-half mile in length. These persist for quite awhile after the ship creating them has passed."

The Search Continues

Tourists, scientists and local folk often make journeys to Loch Ness in search of Nessie. Each wants to be the first to produce the good photograph or movie film that will prove Nessie's existence beyond the shadow of a doubt. But the lake's size and isolation means that a visitor would have to be awfully lucky to be standing at just the right spot, camera in hand, at just the right moment to record a Nessie "guest appearance." The odds against this are vast. Even on those rare occasions when someone has snapped a picture, blurring, distance, or other conditions have kept the pictures from being "proof positive."

What is clearly needed is some kind of a constant "Nessie watch." For based on the reports to date, Nessie shows itself at irregular hours, and then only briefly. A person catches a glimpse, rubs his or her eyes in disbelief, then the creature is gone. Perhaps it was only a mirage, a mistake, or wishful thinking. Or could it have been the real thing, moving quicker than the surprised onlooker can bring a camera into play?

Two

Who Saw Nessie First?

The first reported sighting of Nessie was by Saint Columba, the Irishman who would later be revered for bringing the Christian religion to Scotland. The saint reportedly saw "a water monster" trying to attack a man swimming in Loch Ness. According to the saint's biographer, writing in A.D. 565*, a hundred years later, a huge creature "rushed up with a great roar and open mouth," intent on destruction. But the saint made the sign of the cross in the air and commanded the "fearsome beastie" to go back. At the sound of Saint Columba's voice, the terrified monster "fled more quickly than if it had been pulled back with a rope."

A thousand years after that, a nobleman was hunting near Loch Ness and reportedly killed a strange beast, "without feet, having a fin on one side, a tail, and a terrible head." The beast, believed to be a "dragon," was said to move with great speed. Cameras did not exist at the time, and no proof of

Opposite page: this illustration was drawn from a description by a Dr. Matheson, who spied the creature in 1893. The long neck is one of the most common features mentioned in eyewitness accounts.

*A.D. stands for *Anno Domini*—"Year of Our Lord"— and means that year after the birth of Christ, which is the starting point of the current calender. It is the opposite of B.C.—"Before Christ"—which counts backwards from the date of Christ's birth.

this hunting feat remains.

From that time on, loch beast stories were told by local folk, who often called the creature "Nessie." Stories of an aquatic (water dwelling) monster fit in with local traditions throughout the British Isles. Highlanders talked of *kelpies*, water horses of Scottish rivers, while the Irish spoke of *ech ushkya* (from the Gaelic *eac uisge*), similar beasts that haunted Ireland's lakes and rivers. These could appear as sleek horses, but anyone who mounted them would be carried into a river or loch to drown. The *ech ushkya* were reported to be people-eaters as well. By the 1800s, the topic had become almost a joke, and those who thought they had seen Nessie often kept the information to themselves rather than be laughed at.

Then, on May 2, 1933, the *Inverness Courier*, a local newspaper, carried this huge headline: STRANGE SPECTACLE ON LOCH NESS. The story read,

> On Friday of last week, a well-known businessman, who lives near Inverness, and his wife (a University graduate), when motoring along the north shore of the loch, not far from Abrichan Pier, were startled to see a tremendous upheaval on the loch, which, previously, had been as calm as the proverbial mill-pond. The lady was the first to notice the disturbance, which occurred fully three-quarters of a mile from the shore, and it was her sudden cries to stop that drew her husband's attention to the water.

> There, the creature disported itself, rolling and plunging for fully a minute, its body resembling that of a whale, and the water cascading and churning like a simmering cauldron. Soon, however, it disappeared in a boiling mass of foam. Both onlookers confessed that there was something uncanny about the whole thing, for the beast, in taking the final plunge, sent out waves that were big enough to have been caused by a passing steamer. The watchers waited for almost half-an-hour in the

hope that the monster (if such it was) would come to the surface again: but they had seen the last of it.

Nessie certainly became active in 1933. At least fifty people reported seeing the "black humps" of the enormous creature. One couple even claimed to see it cross the road, slithering quickly between a clump of tall ferns on one side and the dark lake water on the other side of the road. Completely astonished, the couple later mentioned their adventure to a passing bicyclist. "I'm glad you saw it too," the bicyclist said. "A friend of mine saw it, and people at the village have been laughing at him."

One theory for the sudden rash of new sightings was the building of a new road along Loch Ness's north shore. This involved a great amount of blasting, during which large quantities of rock came rolling down the mountain, falling into the water below. The noise and splashing might have so annoyed Nessie that it either awoke from hibernation and became more active, or decided to look at what was happening out of simple curiosity.

"The creature has a series of humps like an upturned boat," most newspapers reported. "Some have said it has a longish neck and a small head. It moves with and without splashing." These same newspapers, looking for increased sales, took to calling Nessie a "monster," a term disliked by local people. To them, Nessie is merely a part of nature, and therefore more correctly called a "beast." But the monster name took the public's fancy, and as widespread interest grew, even more tales appeared in the local papers and began to be picked up in papers throughout the British Isles.

Of course there were plenty of people who did not believe these rumors and reports. "What you saw were seals or porpoises," was the most common way of explaining away Nessie. However, one local newspaper, while keeping the matter of a lake monster an

Miss Janet Fraser of Aultsaye and ten other persons claimed to have seen the monster on September 22, 1933.

open question, did point out that neither seals nor porpoises have ever been known to live in Loch Ness.

A popular theory, still clung to by some die-hard believers, was that it might be a dinosaur that lived in water. The reasoning ran that such a dinosaur might have survived because the lake was so deep it offered protection.

The more skeptical townsfolk were apt to dismiss such ideas as a case of too much imagination. Quite a few curious visitors who had encountered wind and waves, loch and landscape, but had seen not a trace of head or hump, fin or flipper, were inclined to disbelieve such tales. But there were still many visitors, some coming great distances, drawn by the lure of glimpsing a "monster." In fact, it was even suggested that local business people were making up the Nessie stories just to bring in more tourists to local inns, restaurants, and shops.

Many people, with no obvious reason for making up stories, reported seeing Nessie. They included doctors, clergy, farmers, and teachers. An engineer, A.H. Palmer, described the beast's head as follows: "At each side I saw a short antenna which I can best describe as being like the horns on the head of a snail. Between them was a wide mouth opening and closing at two-second intervals." Palmer estimated Nessie's mouth as somewhere between twelve and eighteen inches wide.

A Photograph Is Taken

The debate continued between Nessie's supporters and those who called the matter a joke, a hoax, or an error. Things might have gone on just this way forever, with no real proof offered by either side. But the affair took on a dramatic turn on November 12, 1933, when photographer Hugh Gray produced a photograph of the Loch Ness monster!

Gray's photograph shows a series of ripples on the lake's surface which appear to outline a curving, wormlike shape, narrowing at one end and blunt at

the other. The image suggests a creature that was apparently swimming just below the water's surface.

But publication of this picture did not convince everybody that the Loch Ness monster existed. Immediately, skeptics put forth arguments that denied the picture was proof at all. While photographic experts stated that the picture was genuine, many scientists refused to believe they were looking at the photograph of a living creature. Much of the problem stemmed from the fact that Gray was an amateur photographer using a box camera that produced a blurred image.

One expert from the British Museum of Natural History commented, "I am afraid the photo does not appear to me to be the picture of any living thing.

The Hugh Gray photograph, taken on November 12, 1933. That year was one of the busiest for Nessie sightings.

My personal opinion is that it shows a rotting tree trunk which rises to the loch surface when gas has generated in its cells." Other zoologists, persons who specialize in studying animals, thought it was a shark or perhaps even a whale. While such creatures are usually found in saltwater, they can exist in fresh water for indefinite periods of time. Recently, for example, a humpback whale, nicknamed "Humphrey the wayward whale," swam up California's Sacramento River and had to be steered back to the Pacific Ocean by people worried about its safety. These animals may well be able to adapt entirely to a freshwater environment.

Enter the Hunter

With Nessie being called everything from a monster to a tree trunk to a shark, the riddle of what—if anything—was behind the sightings became even more of a challenge. In an effort to find an answer, and provide its readers an intriguing story that would help sell newspapers, the British *Daily Mail* hired M.A. Wetherell, an African big-game hunter, to search for Nessie. A shock of excitement went through the *Daily Mail's* readership when a December 21, 1933 headline trumpeted "MONSTER OF LOCH NESS IS NOT A LEGEND BUT A FACT." According to the published account, Wetherell had found proof that an amphibian monster, a creature able to breathe on land or water, definitely lived in Loch Ness.

Wetherell, the newspaper delightedly reported, had found four footprints on the western shore of the lake. Being an expert jungle tracker, he claimed he could tell a lot about an animal from its tracks. The footprints, he said, were from an unknown animal. He went on to describe the animal as about twenty feet long and able to breathe with just its nostrils out of water, like a crocodile. Wetherell also stated that the tracks were no more than a few hours old. Nessie

This is the scene most Nessie hunters imagine they will see when the monster appears.

Mr. Alexander Ross claimed to have seen the monster on three occasions in 1933.

was not only alive and well, the beast was able to walk, he asserted.

What had been, up to this point, mainly an item of local interest suddenly exploded into a worldwide mystery. Newspapers around the globe picked up the story just in time for the Christmas holiday.

Back at Loch Ness, plaster casts of the Nessie tracks were made and sent to the British Museum of Natural History. Vacationers trekked to the lake by the thousands. "Monster-hunting parties" were suddenly fashionable, and all the local hotels were filled. Now that there seemed to be real evidence that Nessie existed, each visitor was determined to be the first to see and photograph the beast whose tracks had been found. At about the same time, a circus posted a reward of nearly $40,000 to the person who would bring in the beast, dead or alive—but preferably alive.

A Bounty

That same year, W. Reid Blair, director of the Bronx Zoo in New York City, offered $10,000 to any person capturing the monster and bringing it to New York. The monster had to be alive and healthy on delivery."If there is a Monster in Loch Ness," Blair said, "we want to get it for the New York Zoo. My own belief is that there is some unusual creature in the loch." The rewards only added to the frenzy around Inverness.

But just as the excitement reached fever pitch, the apparent evidence was revealed to be something different. A museum expert testified that all four footprints were identical, and looked exactly like those made by a hippopotamus. Wetherell's great find was a hoax. The tracks turned out to have been made by a mummified hippopotamus foot that had been made into an umbrella stand and was owned by a local resident. Whether the big-game hunter was in on the joke or had been duped himself, he left Loch Ness suddenly, presumably to return to Africa, where underwater monsters and umbrella stands would be just a distant memory.

The *Daily Mail* newspaper, however, became the laughingstock of other newspapers, who soon began treating all further Nessie stories as a joke. Most people now assumed Nessie did not exist and had never existed. They dismissed anybody who thought differently as a publicity hunter at worst, or a bit crazy at best. The hippopotamus foot hoax did tremendous damage to the ongoing search for the Loch Ness monster. Few townsfolk were willing to admit openly that the creature might be real.

Yet even while they kept quiet about it, a few honest, sensible folk continued to believe Nessie made its home in Loch Ness. As time went on, the

"Dr. George Zug of Washington's prestigious Smithsonian said he personally concurred with the interpretation that there are large animate objects in the twenty to thirty foot size range in Loch Ness."

Gerald Snyder, *Is There a Loch Ness Monster?*

"There is no evidence to prove that any of the photographs were of animate creatures or were even of the same object."

Dr. John Shields of Britain's Natural History Museum, quoted in *Is There a Loch Ness Monster?*

This cage was built in 1933 to hold Nessie if he/she/it were ever captured alive.

lake became the most photographed body of water on earth. Dozens of people visited it regularly with their cameras. Every time a fish came to the surface, the camera shutters clicked rapidly, just in case this might be the once-in-a-lifetime sighting that would prove Nessie's existence. Among the thousands of photos taken, two or three actually showed bulky shapes. Many people believed these resembled the monster, but they could not be identified with any certainty.

Loch Ness monster sightings flourished. On the

evening of January 5, 1934, Arthur Grant, a young veterinary student, reported that he was speeding along the loch road on his motorcycle. Suddenly, in the bright moonlight, he saw a dark shape beside the road about forty yards ahead. It lumbered across the road, disappearing into the water with a loud splash. By the time Grant had come to a stop and gone to search, only water ripples were left as evidence of the creature. But the image of what he had seen remained firmly fixed in Grant's mind. He was trained as a veterinarian, and he had studied all kinds of animals. He maintained the creature was certainly unlike any he had ever seen or studied before.

A Lucky Shot

One of the most famous photos, which has continued to stir the most excitement, even though it has been widely denounced as a fake, was taken by a doctor on April 1, 1934. According to the physician, he was driving by the loch early in the morning when he saw an unusual movement on the water. Using a telephoto lens on his camera, he obtained four shadowy shots of what he said was the monster slowly sinking beneath the water. One photograph seemed to show a creature with a long snake-like neck and small head.

The developed photos did not appear to be fakes. However no agreement could be reached on what they really showed. For every person claiming this was truly the monster, there was someone else who said, "Nonsense! It's a long-necked diving bird or a branch or the fin of a large fish."

Skeptics pointed out that the date of the famous photographs, April 1, is April Fool's Day. They suggested that the doctor was playing a joke. Author Henry H. Bauer reported some fifty years later that, "Quite recently it has been claimed that the surgeon admitted to a close friend that his famous photographs were a hoax; and a recent analysis of the most famous photograph reaches a similar conclu-

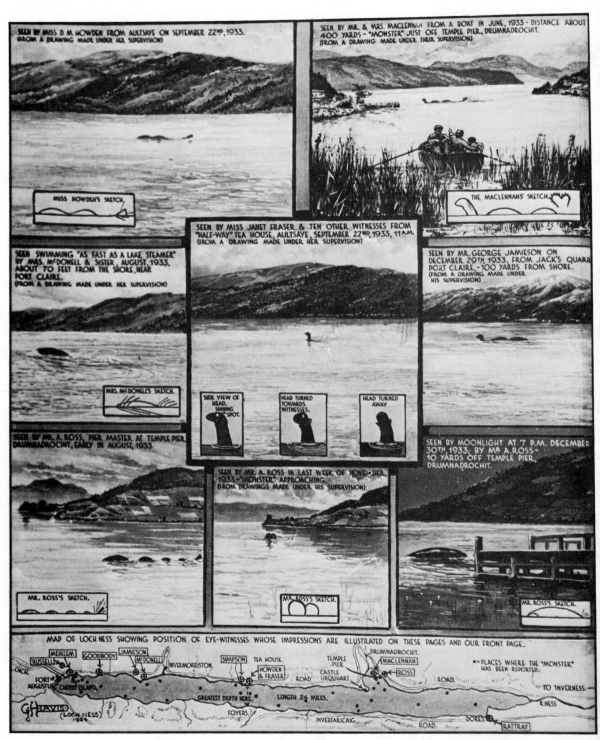

In 1934 *The London News* published these drawings of what locals supposedly saw in the loch. Note the map of Loch Ness at the bottom, detailing each location of a sighting.

sion." Still, this "Surgeon's Photograph" of Nessie remains the best-known to this day, and is constantly reprinted in books and newspapers—inviting readers to make their own decisions.

Monster Watch

In the summer of 1934, not long after the doctor took his photos, a wealthy businessman sponsored the first major expedition to solve the mystery of Loch Ness. Under the direction of Captain James Fraser, who hailed from the town of Inverness at the north end of Loch Ness, twenty townsfolk were hired to help keep a continuous watch on the loch. Each .would now list his or her official occupation as "Watcher for the Monster." Each was given a pair of binoculars and a camera. A cash bonus was promised to anyone who actually photographed Nessie. Each Watcher took up an assigned position around the lake.

The constant monitoring brought some results. Eleven "reasonably clear sightings" were made. There were also five photographs taken showing an unusual object in the lake. One Watcher spotted something in the water that he claimed was "clearly the monster's head which appeared to be like that of a goat. On top of the head were two stumps resembling a sheep's horns broken off." This Watcher also noted the creature had a black or dark brown color, and had smooth skin with lizard-like markings. He added that it had slitted eyes, seemed about twenty feet long, and had flippers on its front. It moved at about eight miles an hour, but did not seem to need its flippers to do this. Nor did it remain in sight for very long. True to form, Nessie dove into the water, leaving a stream of bubbles in its wake.

Of the five photographs taken by "Monster Watchers," on closer investigation, four appeared to be nothing more than disturbances of the lake surface caused by passing boats. A fifth photo, of very poor quality, shows something in the water tossing up spray.

Is Movie Film Proof Enough?

However, Captain Fraser's people weren't working alone. Fraser himself went out regularly to the shores of the lake. He reported that, on an early September morning, Nessie suddenly appeared, as if determined to prove its existence. Captain Fraser turned on his movie camera, managing to catch on film something coming out of the water, giving off a jet of spray, and diving out of sight. Later he reported the dark shape resembled "an upturned, flat-bottomed boat."

There was a great deal of excitement as people waited eagerly for the movie film to be developed. However, what the film clip actually showed was not clear. Some zoologists claimed the photos depicted nothing more than a seal. Momentarily a hero, Captain Fraser became the object of ridicule, and the Monster Watch project soon ended. Local residents generally declined to talk to outsiders about "their" monster. They, too, did not want to be laughed at.

Yet outsiders continued to carry the legend away with them, spreading Nessie's fame. "We were always doubtful about the truth of any Monster existing in Loch Ness," one woman traveller wrote. "But I happened to gaze across the loch and I was amazed to see an object slowly come to the surface." She described the object as black and about eighteen feet long. "Now I have no doubt that there is some living thing here which scientists have not yet been able to explain," she added.

Her report, and those of seemingly reliable witnesses, did succeed in changing the opinions of a few scientists. But the doubts weren't dismissed. To many, Nessie was still a joke. In the months and years that followed, interest in Loch Ness and its monster gradually faded as "hard" evidence—clear photographs, bones, or the capture of the creature itself—eluded the most devoted monster hunters. The world was rushing toward World War II and had more serious problems to worry about. Although some persons continued to believe that a huge unknown creature lived in this remote Scottish lake, by and large Nessie was almost forgotten.

Yet wartime conditions and widespread lack of interest did not stop Nessie from appearing. In 1943, with the war at its peak, a member of the Royal Observer Corps on watch for enemy bombers claimed he saw Nessie through his binoculars. The creature had large bulging eyes, he reported, and a "fin" on its neck. It fed by raising and lowering its head ike a swan. The beast eventually disappeared quietly, leaving not even a ripple behind.

Aside from such infrequent sightings, Nessie largely sank into obscurity—crowded out of the papers by war news and the events of the post-war world. But this was only an "intermission" in one of the most enduring mysteries of the world. Sixteen years later, the question of the existence or non-existence of the Loch Ness monster became the focus of a debate that spread to all corners of the globe.

"If 90 percent of the 10,000 known sightings of the Loch Ness Monster which have been made over the years were shown to be misidentifications of known phenomena, that would still leave 1,000 inexplicable reports."

Janet and Colin Bord, *Alien Animals*

"The reports of sightings have long been dismissed as doubtful. The reports are a striking example of mass hallucinations."

E.G. Boulenger, former aquarium director, London Zoo, quoted in the *New York Times*

Three

Does Loch Ness Have the Only Water Monster?

Opposite page: Jonah was swallowed by a "great fish" in the Bible, one of the first accounts of a monstrous water creature.

Tales of water-dwelling monsters go back as far as written history, and are by no means unique to Loch Ness. Giant beasts of lake, river, and sea have long been part of religious traditions as well as folklore. Their sightings move across time and geography.

The ancient Babylonian people of the Middle East wrote of a dragon called Tiamat who represented the power of the sea and was slain by the god Marduk. African legends also mention sea serpents. The aboriginal Semelai tribe of Malaya had legends of a great serpent that lived in Tasek Bera lake. It closely resembled the Loch Ness monster, including the small horns on its head.

The best known religious story of a water-dwelling monster is Jonah and the "great fish" that swallowed him. The story is popularly referred to as "Jonah and the Whale." The *leviathan*, supposedly the largest monster in creation, was said to be so vast that only the ocean could hold it. In Jewish legend when God saw the power of the two leviathans he had created, he realized the power of these creatures could destroy the world. God destroyed one so that they would not multiply—but made the other immortal as

"Up until now, Nessie has principally been a music-hall joke and a tourist gimmick."

Journalist Thomson Prentice, *The Daily Mail*

"I don't give a damn what some people in the scientific community say. When I make my case to friends of mine who are atomic physicists, they tell me, 'If we had ten percent of this amount of evidence for subatomic particles or black holes, we'd be on much more solid ground."

Roy Mackal, quoted in *Discover* magazine

a sign of his power. That image of the solitary, powerful, undying monster has an echo in the tales of Loch Ness.

Pictures of Viking boats that roamed the seas from A.D. 700 to A.D. 1,000 usually show a fierce dragon or sea serpent head on their prows. Sea serpents were said to be covered with sea-green scales glistening on their upper body and white scales underneath. They had a flattened snake-like head, large eyes and a horse-like mane. Tales were told of sea serpents 228 feet long and twenty-three feet wide.

Viking legends also told of a *kraken,* an enormous devilfish or giant octopus with many tentacles "which grow thicker and thicker the higher they rise above the surface of the water." Sometimes these tentacles reached as high "as the masts of middle-sized vessels." Vikings feared the sight of churning waters, a sign of the kraken's approach.

Old books tell of great "worms" that terrified sailors. As late as 1848, the captain and crew of a British warship sailing in the East Indies reported seeing a sea serpent, its jaws full "of large jagged teeth." The dark brown animal, which resembled a snake, was reputedly at least sixty feet long and sixteen inches wide. It had either a mass of seaweed or a horse's mane on its back.

Modern-day Monsters

Even today, in Sweden, a Great Lake Monster has supposedly been seen many times in Lake Storsjon, in the northernmost section of that country. In 1898, zoologist Dr. Peter Olsson collected twenty-two reports for the years 1820-1898 from trustworthy witnesses. Interestingly, the appearance and behavior of the mystery creature tallied with many of the descriptions coming from Loch Ness and other lakes worldwide. The mystery creature has an "upturned boat shape." It either drifts silently or moves with great speed.

It boasts one or more humps, and its passage is marked by a strong surge of waves possibly caused by the creature swimming just below the water's surface. In present day Sweden, this monster is called *Storsjoowdjure*. Occasionally people have tried to harpoon it, but the creature has always escaped. Other strange, great creatures have been seen in Lake Lilla Kallsjo and Lake Myllesjon.

The *Ahuizotl* is supposedly a creature of the highland lakes of Central America. "No one who sees the Ahuizotl lives to tell the tale," states author Michael Page, "and so any description of the monster is purely imaginary." This monster causes large ripples on a lake, which some guess is due to its tail movements. It has been reputed to tip boats, swallowing the passengers as they fall into the water.

In the the late 1800s, a man named William Buckley dwelled with an aboriginal tribe. He told the story of spotting a gray Lake Modewarre creature with its back covered with feathers. Buckley mentioned that the natives "had a great dread of the lake creatures, believing them to have some supernatural power." The aborigines call it *bunyip*, a tribal term meaning "devil" or "spirit." This bunyip "seemed to be about the size of a full-grown calf, and sometimes larger; the creatures only appear when the weather is very calm and the water smooth," according to Buckley. This is the same sort of weather, especially when accompanied by mists, that Loch Ness residents recognize as "Nessie weather."

Water monsters were reported in the 1950s and 1960s in the Soviet Union at Lake Khaiyr, Lake Vorota, and Lake Labynkyr in Siberia. These have been described as beasts with long and sometimes shiny necks, huge bodies, and an upright back fin. Viewers occasionally saw such creatures on shore, just as Nessie in rare instances has been discovered on the shores of its native loch. According to a report made in 1953 by eyewitness geologist V.A.

"The initial skepticism of the experts, together with improbable claims by witnesses and the occurrence of hoaxes and the connection with sea serpents, quite quickly persuaded the newspapers that Nessie was nothing but a silly-season phenomenon."

Henry Bauer, *The Enigma of Loch Ness*

"Perhaps the case of the Loch Ness Monster will add one more item to the list of zoological absurdities which became realities."

Gerald Snyder, *Is There a Loch Ness Monster?*

Terrifying creatures from the deep have been part of human mythology for centuries.

Tverdokhlebov, the lake creature "had eyes, light-colored patches on the side of its head and a dark gray body. Along its back was a twenty-inch high fin. It moved forward in leaps and at 100 yards from shore it stopped and sent up a great cascade of spray before diving out of sight."

Water Monsters in North America

Eighty-mile-long Lake Okanagan in western Canada has its special monster, called Ogopogo. Multiple reports of its existence appeared in Indian tales prior to the arrival of the first white settlers in 1860. The Indian name was *Na-ha-ha-itkh*, which means "lake demon." Because the beast might attack a canoe, it was best to throw in a pig or chicken first. If Ogopogo appeared for a quick meal, it was considered wisest to make the journey at another time. The creature is said to have devoured a whole herd of horses who were trying to swim across the lake.

Ogopogo is from thirty to seventy feet long, about two feet thick, with a dark sleek body and a horse-shaped head. Reports still occasionally appear, including one from a newspaper editor and another from a water-skier, who got close enough to say that the creature's "blue-gray scales glistened like a rainbow trout as the sun shown on him." For the curious, believers and disbelievers, the Canadians have built a huge statue of Ogopogo on the shores of Lake Okanagan. Creatures of similar description have been seen in Canada's lakes Manitoba, Dauphin, and Winnipegosis.

The United States has its share of water monsters too. In Montana, early Indian legends told of a monster dwelling in Flathead Lake. In 1885, a steamboat captain operating on this lake thought he saw another boat coming toward him. Instead, according to reports, it turned out to be a large animal similar to a whale. He fired on it, and it dove under water. In 1960, visitors to a lakeside country club heard some-

Another typical description of Nessie includes humps or parts of its body that break the surface much like the motion of an eel or snake.

thing scratching itself against a pier. They went for a closer look. The woman reported, "It was a horrible looking thing, with a head about the size of a horse and about a foot of neck showing." She screamed, and the creature swam away very rapidly.

The first recorded sighting on Lake Champlain (which straddles the American-Canadian border) was by the French explorer Samuel de Champlain. In 1609 he wrote notes about a serpentine creature, twenty feet long, thick as a barrel and with a head like a horse. In 1945, while rowing on the portion of Lake Champlain that extends into Vermont, a Vermont husband and wife came close enough to a similar creature "to whack it with an oar." The same year, passengers and crew of the S.S. Ticonderoga, spectators at a bridge-opening ceremony, saw a strange head rise above the water. In 1971, a Mrs. Robert Green reported a snaky head and three black humps gliding through the water. There have been so many sightings on this lake that the beast has been given the name "Champ."

In 1970, in Southern California, an area resident reported seeing a twelve-foot snake-like creature swimming in Lake Elsinore. Checking out this wild report, three officials from Elsinore State Park went out in a boat. The creature, or whatever unusual object it might have been, appeared just fifty feet from them.

Returning to the British Isles, in the Connemara region of Ireland, there is a 1986 sighting by a local farmer. He claimed that his wife, and five children

"There are not enough small fish in the lake to support a monster."

Scientist Adrien J. Desmond, quoted in *Sea Monsters*

"There are plenty of fish in the lake."

Professor Hubert Colchester, *Sea Monsters*

Strange sea monsters roamed the oceans as depicted in medieval sailing charts.

stood twenty feet away from a twelve-foot-long creature swimming around their local Lake Nahooin. It was "an animal with a pole-like head and neck about nine inches to a foot in diameter," Farmer Coyne reported. "From time to time it put its head underwater; two humps then came into view. Occasionally, a flat tail appeared. The thing was black, slick and hairless, with a texture resembling an eel." Mrs. Coyne mentioned it had two horn-like projections on top of its head. Neither person saw any eyes or teeth on the creature.

Do Other Scottish Lakes Have Monsters?

In Scotland, huge water beasts aren't limited to Loch Ness. When Duncan MacDonnell and William Simpson were heading home after a day's boat fishing on Loch Morar, southwest of Loch Ness,

The enormous size of Loch Ness has permitted Nessie believers to insist that the monster is naturally difficult to spot in such a huge body of water.

MacDonnell heard a splashing to the boat's side. "I looked up," he said afterward, "and saw this creature coming directly after us in our wake. It soon grazed the side of the boat. I am quite certain this was unintentional."

MacDonnell grabbed an oar and attempted to push the creature away. When the oar broke, Simpson grabbed his rifle and shot at the creature. It slowly sank away from the boat.

The year was 1969 and the pair got a good look at their unwelcome visitor. "I don't want to see it again," Simpson said. "I was terrified." The monster they described was thirty feet long, had rough, dirty brown skin, three humps projecting eighteen inches out of the water, and a brown foot-wide snake-like head. It is easy to understand why the men were terrified.

The account attracted the attention of several biologists. The following year they set up a watch team along the shore and began interviewing area residents. They discovered that over thirty-three detailed reports had been made about "Morag" the monster between 1887 and 1971.

Mystery beast sightings have also occurred in recent years at Loch Tay. Loch Ness, Loch Morar, and Loch Tay are all in remote areas. All three are extremely deep lakes. Perhaps they offer similar environments and have become home to similar creatures.

Are The Witnesses Reliable?

On the other hand, it is possible that all the above stories are merely legends that began with the observation of some less exotic sea creature or a bit of imagination. From this, stories somehow grew with the passing of time. It is possible that all persons making the reports had a bit too much to drink, were overtired, didn't see well, or were a bit daft. It is even possible to argue that all the people lied for one reason or another, including wanting the publicity that newspaper reports can bring. Sea monster reports might also be a combination of some or all of the above.

Yet many witnesses appear to be highly reliable people with no apparent reason for exaggeration of any kind. Some have been slow to come forth for fear of being thought foolish or overly imaginative. The sheer number of reports coming from areas around the world is impressive. The similarity of details is also interesting. Some people are quick to suggest that people who make such reports have already been told by newspaper or television accounts what to expect to see. But this explanation disregards many long-ago reports when information had no way of travelling from one country to another.

While reports might not all be true, some or many may be true. The monsters in other lakes could possibly have survived from a prior age, just as Nessie might have. So many of the above descriptions do seem to be talking about the same type of animal. Could these be Nessie's cousins? And just what sort of fish, mammal, reptile, or other creature might Nessie be?

Four

What Type of Creature Is Nessie?

Almost everybody who hears about Nessie takes a guess as to what it might really be.

Is Nessie a Mammal?

Accusations have been made that Nessie is no monster or strange beast, but really a very ordinary whale, stranded sea cow, or seal.

Nessie has been reported to be from fifteen to sixty feet long. Whales, reaching up to 100 feet, would certainly fit the size description. Whales are wonderful swimmers and divers. They could live comfortably in the cold water of Loch Ness. And some whales are fish eaters, although the majority live off of krill—a tiny form of sea life that whales filter from seawater they take in and eject. There are plenty of fish in the lake.

But whales are the wrong shape, since most descriptions of Nessie stress a long neck and small head. Moreover whales have never been observed taking a stroll. The Loch Ness creature has reportedly been seen several times on land. Whales must come to the water's surface to breathe at regular intervals. This would make them visible a good part of the day. Nessie certainly does not seem to come to the sur-

Fort Augustus, at the south end of Loch Ness. Does a family of giant eels
live in the deep Scottish lake?

face unless it appears to be in the mood.

What about seals? They swim quickly, eat fish, and prefer cold water. While a seal's head is small and its neck short while swimming, it can stretch outward when seeking food, appearing to have a medium-size neck. But our knowledge of seal habits rules them out, even though elephant seals are large enough to be small Nessies. Seals like to sun themselves on shore. Their pups are born on land. If seals were the Loch Ness creatures, they would be on shore during every breeding season, and would be making so much noise that everybody would know exactly who and where they were. Again, while it is possible in theory for a seal to have come up the river that runs from Loch Ness into the North Sea, none has been observed attempting this. And, as was mentioned above, there is no report of seals ever having been sighted in the loch.

"Maybe it is a Stellar's sea cow," some suggest. Long ago, sea cows used to be quite long, maybe reaching thirty feet. An adult might weigh more than eight thousand pounds. All that blubber was topped with a comparatively tiny head. When in deep water, a Stellar's sea cow floated with its head and tail hanging down and its back in a humped position. Sea cows also had a shoulder hump. When a mother carried her calf on her back, it made her seem two-humped. Many Nessie sightings include mention of a hump, so a huge sea cow seems a natural guess.

Descriptions of a Stellar's sea cow's face also seem to fit the Nessie picture. "The skull is not too different in its general shape from a horse's skull; when it is still covered with flesh and hide it resembles a buffalo's head," says author Roy Mackal. Witnesses have also claimed that Nessie has "a head and face the size of a large dog," "a horse-like face," "a face about the size of a cow's head," and a "giraffe-like" head and neck.

But sea cows were extinct by 1761, killed off by

hunters. And even if one or more survived the ocean slaughter by hiding (there are occasional unverified reports of sea cow sightings as late as the 1960s), there are problems here too. Sea cows are air breathers, like whales. They would have to make many visible visits to the lake's surface. Another negative is the fact that plants were their food supply. Plants are in short supply in the gloomy loch. And with their inability to move about on land, this just about rules them out.

Is Nessie a Turtle?

While those who have described Nessie certainly don't sound as if they are talking about a turtle, the possibility has been mentioned more than once.

A turtle has a long neck and a small head. It swims and dives easily. What was taken as a hump might just as easily be a curved shell. Turtles eat fish, and turtles can walk on land. It sounds almost perfect, except for a few facts.

Turtles do not grow to sixty feet or even to fifteen feet. The largest gets only ten feet long, and reaches a mere two thousand pounds. That is quite a small Nessie. Nor are all turtles keen on cold water, although the Leatherback turtle shows some ability to adapt to varying temperature. Turtles breathe air and they certainly would be noticed often enough with their long necks sticking out above the water.

Is Nessie a Salamander?

Frogs and toads have never been considered as possible Loch Ness monsters because they are much too small and the wrong shape. But today's giant salamanders, found in Japan, can reach a maximum of 100 pounds and grow to five feet long. Salamander ancestors were once up to sixteen feet long, some 250 million years ago.

Author Roy Mackal, a dedicated Nessie searcher, has made a careful study of all the reported sightings. He has also investigated the backgrounds of

This mini-sub appears much like the sea monster it is meant to find. This underwater approach to spy Nessie was attempted by Dan Taylor in 1969.

large animals reputed to live in the loch. After going through all available information, Mackal has concluded that the loch creatures are "giant amphibians thought to be extinct for 250 million years." Has an ancient salamander found its home in Loch Ness waters? It is not as popular a theory as whales or seals or even turtles, because salamanders are not very glamorous creatures. But they like cold fresh water and eat almost anything, and some can breathe under water for long periods. In addition, salamanders have long tails and long bodies, and the young have a frilly back fin. Their body gills, sticking out from the head, might even be mistaken for Nessie's often reported "horns."

Most folk disputing the salamander theory immediately say, "But they have short necks and big heads. Nessie has a long neck and a little head." True enough. Nevertheless, a salamander survivor from the past remains a possible answer to the question, "What type of creature is Nessie?"

Suppose Nessie's an Eel?

In 1954, a local newspaper headline read "The Loch Ness Mystery—Is Nessie Really A Giant Eel?" Eels have always been a mystery. They change shapes, colors, and sizes as they grow. For a long time nobody knew what a baby eel looked like, because it resembles a transparent leaf. Some eels travel thousands of miles from inland freshwater rivers to the salty Atlantic Ocean, breeding there in great numbers and then dying. Their young drift back on the currents to the rivers from which their parents first came.

Freshwater eels live in Loch Ness. It is an ideal place, with its cold water and ample supply of food. Eels eat almost anything, living and dead. While preferring to stay in water, they can and do travel on land, often overcoming amazing obstacles. They also poke their small heads and parts of their long upper bodies out of the water while swimming a wavy, snake-like fashion.

So far, so good. Even better, eels have a long back fin plus two fins on the front part of their bodies that just might be mistaken for Nessie's flippers. When an eel swims on its side, as they sometimes do, it appears to have humps. Nessie has humps. And, like the reported Loch Ness beast, eels swim rapidly and can dive from sight in a matter of seconds.

But nothing's perfect, and neither is the eel theory. Eels, as we know them, simply do not come in a large enough size to qualify as a Nessie. The largest eel ever discovered was only ten feet long, and weighed about one hundred pounds. The average

"The Loch Ness Mystery—Is Nessie Really a Giant Eel?"

Headline in *The Scottish Daily Herald* (1954)

"There is nothing to prove Nessie is an eel. Yet the possibility of eel monsters cannot be ruled out."

Gerald Snyder, *Is There A Loch Ness Monster?*

58

> "Just about all the experts now agree the monster is not a gigantic plesiosaur from the Mesozoic Era. Nor is it a giant newt or a great worm."
>
> Journalist James M. Perry, *The Wall Street Journal*

> "The more doubt and cold water that are cast on the likelihood of a latter-day plesiosaur swimming nearby, the more it seems that people want to believe."
>
> Journalist Ronald Faux, *London Times*

size is three feet long. However, author Roy Mackal states there is "the possibility of large, thick-bodied eels in Loch Ness." But that remains to be proven.

Is Nessie a Snail Without a Shell?

Most of us are familiar with land slugs, those relatives of the snail that lack a visible shell. Land slugs do not grow very large, but their sea-dwelling cousins can reach two feet long and a weight of fifteen pounds. A slug can stretch its body out almost double its humped-up size

Some sea slugs have bristles, which help them move, and head growths which might be mistaken for feelers or horns. Descriptions of Nessie have included a slimy appearance, shape changes, horns, and one person even mentioned seeing hair on its head.

While giant sea slugs don't make a very exciting Nessie, they have been considered as a part of the ever-growing list of "maybes." But sea slugs don't move about on land at all, and freshwater slugs aren't very large

Is Nessie a Prehistoric Creature?

Once upon a time, more than 70 million years ago, twenty- to fifty-foot-long plesiosaurs swam about in the warm, shallow seas that covered the earth. They were reptiles related to the dinosaur. A great number of witnesses who have reported seeing Nessie have described a creature that sounds very similar to the plesiosaur.

Plesiosaurs had long, sharp teeth for catching fish. Their necks bent easily, and they propelled themselves with their flippers. One interesting fact about these creatures is that fossils have shown they had "stomach stones." These might have been used to help grind up food the way some birds keep gravel in their gizzards. Some people think that these stones in the bellies of Nessies might make a dead creature sink to the bottom of the loch. This, they say, would explain the absence of bodies or bones on

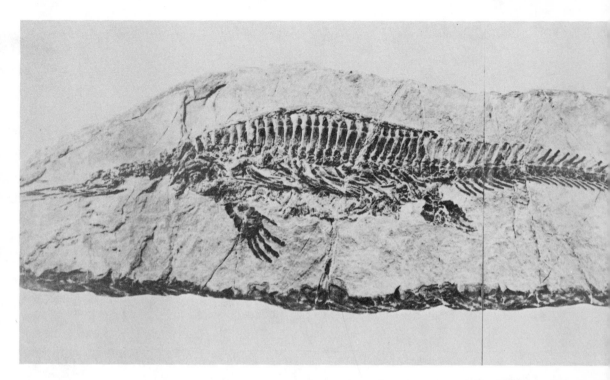

the surface or shore.

While plesiosaurs were predominantly saltwater creatures, their fossils have sometimes been found in fresh water where rivers meet the sea. Moreover, some forms of plesiosaur are believed to have given birth to live young, allowing them to remain underwater most of the year rather than go on shore for breeding purposes.

To some, plesiosaurs are a perfect solution to the riddle of Nessie. Even drawings, reconstructed from fossil finds, look like the Loch Ness creature. Is it possible a few survived, making their home in the Scottish lakes?

Doubters of the plesiosaur theory point out that while plesiosaur fossils have been found, no traces of Nessie have ever been discovered. If Nessie existed, its fossils would have been found too. Doubters also point out that the last of the plesiosaurs was supposed

One theory says that Nessie is descended from a species of prehistoric reptile, or the plesiosaurs from the age of dinosaurs. This fossil here shows a huge reptilian creature 180 million years old.

Could this be the neck of a plesiosaur? Many Nessie hunters feel the species
could have survived in the isolation of Loch Ness.

to have died out some 70 million years ago.

Yet Loch Ness is a good hiding place with its deep waters and underwater crevices and shelves. Yes, plesiosaurs did have to come up to breathe, but if they have survived all this time, maybe they have learned to breathe just at the water's edge, where nobody can see them.

The Tully Monster

There is no guess too strange for Nessie. The writer F.W. Holiday has stated that the Loch Ness creature is a giant *Tullimonstrum gregarium*, or Tully-monster, known only from fossils. The fossils aren't easy to figure out. Tully-monsters might be worms, shellfish, or some totally unknown species.

Tully-monsters were water-dwelling worm-like creatures reaching up to fourteen inches long. They had long skinny necks and tiny heads on one end, and a wide, arrow-shaped tail on the other. There were also two small flipper-like attachments on either side. Of all the creatures mentioned above, the Tully-monster looks most like the Nessie descriptions, except much, much smaller. The major problem here is that the creature disappeared from the earth 380 million years ago. At least that's what scientists think.

A few creatures, such as the ocean-dwelling coelacanth fish, presumed extinct for 70 million years, have been discovered quite alive today. They grow up to seven feet long. A specimen was hauled up in a fisherman's net off the east coast of Africa in 1938.

And consider the *Vampiroteuthis infernalis* fish, resembling a cross between an octopus and a giant squid. Or the *Neopilina galathea* shellfish, part snail and part clam. Scientists thought these strange-looking creatures had been extinct for 350 million years. They were obviously mistaken, as specimens still occasionally show up in the nets of Russian deep sea fishermen.

If these creatures can survive, there might be others. Perhaps Nessie?

"I tend to think it's a seal."
Electronics expert Darrel Lowrance, quoted in the *Los Angeles Times*

"It's not a mammal. Otherwise we would have found its bones. It may be a giant eel."
Field Director Adrian Shine, quoted in *The Wall Street Journal*

Five

The Monster Search Starts Again

The revival of serious study of the Loch Ness was largely due to the publication in 1957 of *More Than a Legend* by Constance Whyte. The author had made a careful investigation of all the known data regarding Nessie—from the earliest folktales through interviews with those who had reported sightings to scientific speculation on the possible nature of the beast. Whyte also made the suggestion that there might be a number of Nessies—a herd cut off from the North Sea during the Ice Age.

Her book sparked the imagination of a new generation of monster hunters. One was English engineer Tim Dinsdale. In 1960 he managed to take a picture of Nessie swimming.

Dinsdale had spent many months at the lake shore trying to capture a picture of the elusive Loch Ness monster. One afternoon his patience paid off. While scientists continued scoffing at "the idea of a real Loch Ness Monster," Dinsdale's photograph, taken with a movie camera, 16 millimeter film, and a telephoto lens, showed a picture of a moving object at least six feet wide and five feet high, with a hump at least twelve feet long. "As it proceeded westward,"

hotograph was taken near Achnahannet in September 1983 by a bicyclist. The mysterious shape, or neck, appeared to be smooth and dark brown, but vanished within seconds.

Tim Dinsdale, hunting for
Nessie, 1969.

he later said, "I watched successive rhythmic bursts of foam break the surface—*paddle strokes*. With such a regular beat I instinctively began to count—one, two, three, four—pure white blobs of froth contrasting starkly against the surrounding black water."

British Royal Air Force photography experts from the Joint Air Reconnaissance Intelligence Center examined and studied the photograph. Yes, it definitely showed a huge "living thing" in the water. This thing was slightly rounded, triangular shaped, and apparently moving up to ten miles per hour. It had a body part sticking about three feet out of the water.

Dinsdale's film was shown on British television.

Suddenly the world stopped laughing and started to pay serious attention to Nessie again, after a gap of almost twenty years. But the Dinsdale film was too grainy, taken from too great a distance, to put an end to the Loch Ness controversy. It showed something, but what type of some thing? Skeptics still abounded, including one person (not named) who saw the film and commented that the "wake and wash in the film were not inconsistent with those that would be produced by a dinghy [rubber life raft] with an outboard engine." Was Dinsdale's Nessie merely a boat?

Another Monster Watch

Determined to move Nessie into a strictly scientific world, where its existence could be thoroughly proven, the non-profit Loch Ness Phenomenon Investigation Bureau (LNPIB) was formed in 1960. The four founding members were David James, former British naval officer and Member of Parliament, author Constance Whyte, and naturalists Sir Peter Scott and Richard Fitter.

Members of the LNPIB were farmers, school teachers, housewives, students, and business and trades people. These amateur naturalists took turns living in vans on the lake shore. They were equipped with binoculars, note pads, and movie cameras with telephoto lenses. Large searchlights shone on the lake at night, just in case the creature might be curious or attracted to bright lights. Their vigils began at 4:00 a.m. and continued, as one member said, "as long as we could stand up." This often was about 10:00 p.m. "You just sit and stare, run your eyes over the water, mutter to yourself if you like, but that's about all you can do," one watcher said.

The LNPIB put up signs all around the lake: "Any members of the general public who genuinely believe they have seen an unusual creature or object in or on the shores of Loch Ness are requested to report the occurrence to Expedition Headquarters at

> "When the huge number of eyewitness reports is considered we wonder yet again at the refusal of scientists to acknowledge that there is anything unknown which requires to be investigated."
>
> Janet & Colin Bord, *Alien Animals*

> "Reported sightings are far too infrequent, brief, and uninformative to make it reasonable for a scientist to spend at Loch Ness the time needed for the activities of his career."
>
> Henry Bauer, *The Enigma of Loch Ness*

Achnahannet." Headquarters had been set up about two miles south of Urquhart Castle. At this central site, LNPIB members collected reports of "sightings." Whatever pictures the LNPIB members obtained were sent directly to the British Air Ministry in London for expert interpretation. While no provable results were obtained, the LNPIB published newsletter updates, passed out literature about its work, exhibited its cameras, and helped searchers carry out their own expeditions.

Cambridge University scientists appeared in 1962, using sensitive *echosounders* , sonar devices used to determine the depth of a body of water or an underwater object. The theory was that the echosounder beams would annoy any large water creatures so much they would come to the surface where they could be seen. Unfortunately, all that came to the surface were large salmon. At least, that's all that could be proven. One of the Cambridge observers stated he saw a moving "pole-like" object in the loch. But he didn't have his camera available. Cameras do seem to disappear when Nessie shows its hump or any other part.

After a year without any verifiable sightings, the monster watchers became impatient. The records showed that Nessie had been most active when nearby roads were being blasted out in the 1930s. If blasting made Nessie nervous, or aroused its interest, then blast they would. Dynamite explosions soon shook the lake. In 1963, the beast was seen forty times.

In a letter to Dinsdale, noted fishing writer and monster investigator F.W. Holiday wrote, "When people are confronted by this fantastic animal at close quarters, they seem to be stunned. There is something strange about Nessie that has nothing to do with size or appearance." Holiday stated his personal reaction after reviewing records of all the reported sightings was a "mixture of wonder, fear and repulsion."

Author Roy P. Mackal, the longtime Loch Ness investigator and member of the LNPIB, complained that the constant sightings combined with lack of concrete proof caused the group much problem with the press. The media, in turn, created other problems. Headlines such as "Scientists Say Loch Ness Monster Could Be Caught with a Giant Hot Plate" made mockery of the many methods used to locate the creature . "In sixteen of the nineteen newspaper stories," Mackal writes, "my use of the scientific word 'animal' was changed to 'monster.' If I used the figure twelve, it became 1,200. If I said fifty-five feet, it became fifty-five tons." Naturally the public became confused.

High Technology Is Introduced

But the investigations continued. The next scientific instrument used was sonar, first tried at Loch Ness in 1968 under the direction of Professor D. Gordon Tucker, chairman of the Department of Electronic and Electrical Engineering at the University of Birmingham, England.

The sonar was mounted on shore and also towed from boats. Sonar devices send out a sound pulse which bounces off any object in its path. The echo is then recorded on special machines. Sonar is able to track schools of whales, dolphins, and fish. It records the speed and size of objects and the angle they are moving through the water. Sonar is also used to track submarines. It therefore should be able to track the elusive Loch Ness monster.

That same year, the Birmingham team claimed it had succeeded in pinpointing Nessie. Its sonar was able to track a large moving object near the lake bottom. This object was travelling at about 100 feet per minute. No fast-moving current could account for this speed. The scientists were barely able to control their excitement. Another sonar echo trace followed. Then a third. This one was travelling at 450 feet per

Many scholars come to Loch Ness every year for a chance to spot the Loch Ness monster. This history professor from Geneva, Switzerland, came to look for the creature on his camping holiday.

minute, faster than any fish living in the lake could swim. What could it be? The scientists saw nothing on the surface. But Professor Tucker said their sonar results definitely came from "a number of large, animate [living] objects."

A prominent science magazine, *Nature*, called the results misleading. In an editorial entitled "Monsters by Sonar" the magazine stated that Tucker's sonar gear had been tested by a fisheries laboratory and found to be somewhat unreliable. "There is little reason to take seriously the claims" that Professor Tucker and his associate Dr. Braithwaite have found a monster, the magazine stated.

Rebuttals came fast and furious. The gear that Tucker used on Loch Ness had never been tested by the fisheries laboratory, although a very early model of the same machine had. Why the magazine decided to attack the project has never been made clear. Perhaps being negative about Nessie sold magazines. Perhaps, as author Nicholas Witchell surmises, "Once again one sees the scientific establishment desperately trying to defend its territory from the possibility that something exists which it cannot understand."

Scuba divers went down in the cold water. Once again the peat-stained waters defeated efforts to see clearly—let alone photograph anything. Nessie, if it existed, remained safely hidden in the inky depths and distances.

But true believers would not give up the quest for a living air- or water-breathing creature. The following year, scientist Don Taylor from Atlanta, Georgia tried using a small submarine called the *Viperfish* to find Nessie. The *Viperfish*, whose expedition was sponsored by the LNPIB, carried twin biopsy harpoons mounted on an airgun in an attempt to get tissue samples from Nessie's huge body. While Taylor was able to see something on his radar screen, whatever it was moved too quickly for his small underwater ship. And he certainly couldn't see more than a few feet out of the submarine's windows. The lake waters remained oppressively dark and Nessie-free. The *Viperfish* not only failed to obtain Nessie evidence, but its pressure hatch opened under water, almost drowning its crew.

When the news got out that some monster watcher was thinking of spearing Nessie, who had quite a fan club by now, members of the British Parliament voiced their opposition. "Would you like to be 'potted' by an airgun?" Parliamentary member Lord Hawke asked Lord Hughes, the Joint Parliamentary Under-Secretary for Scotland.

"The photographs lead us to believe that the object is animate with proportionally large appendages and either a long neck and head or a long tail."

New England Aquarium chairman David B. Stone quoted in *Is There a Loch Ness Monster?*

"We believe that none of the 1975 photographs is sufficiently informative to prove the existence, far less the identity of a large living animal."

London's Natural History Museum senior zoology staff conclusion

One of the most sophisticated investigations in recent years was undertaken by the Academy of Applied Science under the supervision of Dr. Robert Rines. Rines is shown on these pages adjusting one of the sensitive cameras and lights used to try and photograph the creature underwater.

Lord Hughes replied that if he were Nessie's size, he probably wouldn't notice a piece of flesh missing. However he was challenged by yet another member of Parliament who stated, "Are you aware that it will be an act of sacrilege to take away from the Scottish Tourist Board the myth of the Loch Ness monster by which they get many gullible tourists each year?" True enough, if Nessie did turn out to be a large salmon or salamander, a lot of local business would be lost.

Lord Hughes, a Nessie believer, was offended. "I do not know," he said briskly, "on what scientific grounds my noble friend says the monster is a myth." So the argument raged on, even in the highest political places.

Yet if Nessie's existence could not be proven, the year 1969 was not a total failure in the monster watch. Sonar on a surface boat tracked a large ani-

"But could a whole population of giant undulating reptiles survive undetected for centuries? Not unless they were tiny—and 200 reporters would hardly rush to cover the search for a Loch Ness midget."

The New York Times editorial

"These are probably creatures that man has never seen before. They can be an overgrown version of something or other that we might know of; they could also be prehistoric."

Photographer Dr. Charles Wyckoff, quoted in the *London Times*

mal deep down in the lake waters. As the sonar echo bounced off it, the creature moved ever closer to the boat, though below the surface. The investigators saw nothing. Nessie still seemed to be shy.

"Many scientists still denied there were large animals in Loch Ness," author Ian Thorne writes. During the 1969 filming of *The Private Life of Sherlock Holmes* a fake five-ton moveable monster was made as a prop. During its film debut, it filled with water and promptly sank to the loch's bottom. "That's your monster!" people laughed on hearing the story.

But the scoffers were becoming rapidly outnumbered by the people who were now willing to speak out again and say Nessie did exist. They claimed there was photographic and sonar proof, as well as witnesses.

Americans love adventure, and they were not about to let Britain keep Nessie all to itself.

The Academy of Applied Science, a Boston-based educational institution whose purpose is to support unusual research, sent out a research team. They used sonar echoes to map the bottom of Loch Ness. These echoes demonstrated that there were several underwater caves large enough to hide large animals. *The New York Times* newspaper sent out its reporters and gave monetary support to the Academy.

The Academy of Applied Science institution was directed by lawyer-engineer Robert Rines, working with Dr. Martin Klein, a New Hampshire sonar expert. In 1970, Klein's sonar picked up echoes indicating large objects were in the lake. They did not seem to be fish. Another survey by an Academy group, on another loch site, again picked up "extraordinarily large blips," author Gerald Snyder writes. "These seemed to be something other than fish." From then on, the Americans were part of the monster hunt, sending more investigators each year.

Also climbing onto the publicity wagon was the Scottish whisky firm of Cutty Sark. In 1971, it offered $2.4 million for the monster's capture. The company required that the beast be captured without using poison, explosives, or electrical devices. Cutty Sark wanted Nessie to be "alive and well." Any living trophy had to be at least twenty feet long and verified as the Monster by the curator of the Natural History Museum in London.

While a lot of people wrote for information on the contest, the only person to put in a claim for the reward was a Mississippi woman who said, according to Gerald Snyder, that the "real Monster was her husband of twenty-seven years, and she needed the money to pay for a divorce."

Genuine monster hunters didn't find this at all funny. How could serious investigations be made when people kept treating the subject as a publicity stunt or a joke? Worse, they kept on making false reports which took up researchers' valuable time. David James, one of the founders of LNPIB, said that while he understood why the whisky maker wanted to "cash in on this really rather extraordinary story," he would have been much happier if they put their cash toward scientific research "rather than gimmickry."

Protecting Nessie

James wrote to the Secretary of State for Scotland stating that he was worried about Nessie. Perhaps Scotland should change its 1882 Preservation of Animals Act so that it protected cold-blooded creatures as well as warm-blooded creatures, since they had no "idea whether we're dealing with a warm- or cold-blooded creature."

James's rationale was that no one knew how many monsters there were in the lake. If Nessie were the only one, or the only breeding female, and if it were damaged or killed, the whole species would be wiped out. The world would lose the opportunity to

The Academy of Applied Science team lowers an underwater camera into Urquhart Bay.

see and study a potential marvel. While no action was taken by Scotland's government at that time, public sympathy clearly sided with James. The citizens around Loch Ness had become positively fond of their monster. And, along with sentimentality came the reality that the "monster" was big business. There were even a number of books for children telling all about Nessie. They included photographs of the Loch Ness monster.

In 1972, the Academy of Applied Science used sonar echo to track a living object moving through the lake. The "object" was from twenty to thirty feet long. What was it? The scientists took many underwater pictures. But they still called it an "object." While the pictures showed some vague form, there wasn't enough photographic evidence to confirm that the object was an animal. The loch's cloudy water continued to make underwater photography a difficult job, even with the most up-to-date underwater flash cameras.

The only people regularly reporting sightings of Nessie now were the captains and crew of the commercial fishing ships that roamed the lake. "The electronic fish finder on my boat," said Captain Alex Knot, "has spotted an underwater animal on more than one trip through the lake. Once we were able to stay over the beast for eighteen minutes. It was at a depth of fifty-two feet, moving at six miles per hour, had a length of twenty-four feet, six inches, and was shaped like an eel."

Once again the the monster watchers pointed to the similarities between many of the Nessie sightings: humps, large size, dark gray color, long neck, small head. Surely, the argument ran, so much consistency must show a basis in fact. But skeptics just as tirelessly reminded believers that ever since 1933 people have known from newspaper reports and drawings how the monster was supposed to look, and therefore naturally "see" the same thing.

What was still needed was proof positive: Nessie posing for a full-length, unmistakably clear photograph. And although the LNPIB closed its research in 1972 due to lack of money, in the same year an Academy of Applied Science underwater camera took a picture that was said to be unmistakable evidence for Nessie's existence. Was the search finally over?

Six

Is The Search Over?

Opposite page: *Nessitera rhombopteryx*. This underwater photograph was taken by the Academy of Applied Science (AAS) expedition in June, 1975. The appearance is strikingly like that of the Nessie of legend: small head, long neck and a large body with flippers. Has Nessie been verified at last?

Nessie was found twice in 1972. Once by a group of pranksters, the other by an Academy of Applied Science underwater camera which obtained pictures of its right hind flipper.

Of the two, the flipper was of the most scientific importance, but the prank is best remembered. It started when a group of people from Yorkshire Zoo announced they had found a mysterious monster washed up near the town of Foyers and were taking its body away for investigation. Newspaper headlines were large, television news cameras rushed to the spot, and police roadblocks were set up to prevent anybody from removing Nessie. One of the roadblocks caught the zoo workers carting around a dead elephant-seal with its whiskers cut off and its mouth stuffed with cotton to make it look fuller. The next day's newspaper headlines made anybody who believed in a true Nessie look like a fool.

While all this was happening, the Academy sent its photos to Eastman Kodak in the United States. The Kodak staff signed statements that none of the films had been tampered with. From here, the pictures went to N.A.S.A. computer enhancement

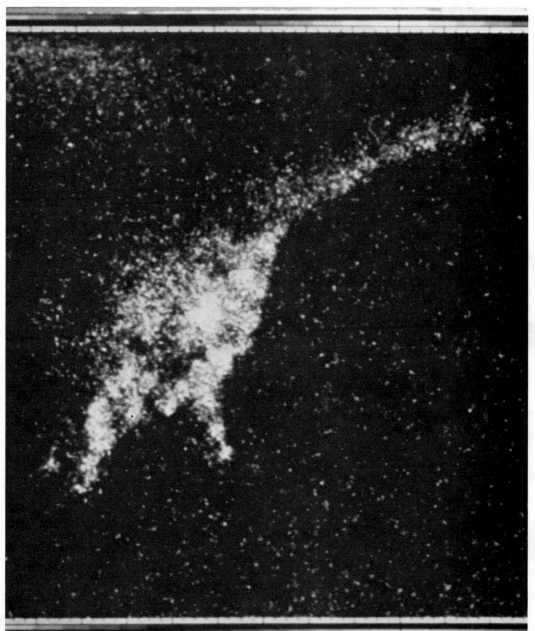

R 1975 - 9/3M SCAN AT 10 MICRONS - FR 1

-149

experts. One photograph stood out from the rest: a flipper-like part joined to a rough-textured body. This was examined by some of the world's leading experts on sonar, photoanalysis and marine zoology. While judgment was cautious, there was general agreement that a large moving object was shown. However, according to Dr. J.G. Sheals, Keeper of Zoology at the Natural History Museum, "Information in the photographs is insufficient to enable identification."

Three years later, the Academy of Applied Science got a better photo of Nessie—its "main body structure" complete with "the head, neck, and body," and possibly front flippers.

And what could be better than a close-up? The same group, the same camera unit, managed to obtain what they termed a close-up photo of Nessie's head. This showed its open mouth, nostril marks above the upper lip, and two horn-like tubes sticking out of its head. "We've got it," Academy of Applied Sciences president Robert Rines said. "We've hit the jackpot!" He called a lawyer friend, Nicholas Witchell, who had once helped him search for Nessie.

"The search is over!" claimed author Witchell upon viewing the pictures. He rushed right away to do another book about the Loch Ness Monster, claiming the world was going to soon see "one of the greatest and most dramatic discoveries of the twentieth century." The hunt would be over, the mystery solved, and everybody would know every detail of Nessie's strange life. Even the scientific world would be "ablaze with excitement."

Truly, many scientists were excited. The "head" was not well lit in any picture and all interpretation had to be done based on shadows cast by the strobe light. But whatever the photograph was showing, it was undeniably a strange object. Or perhaps even a strange creature.

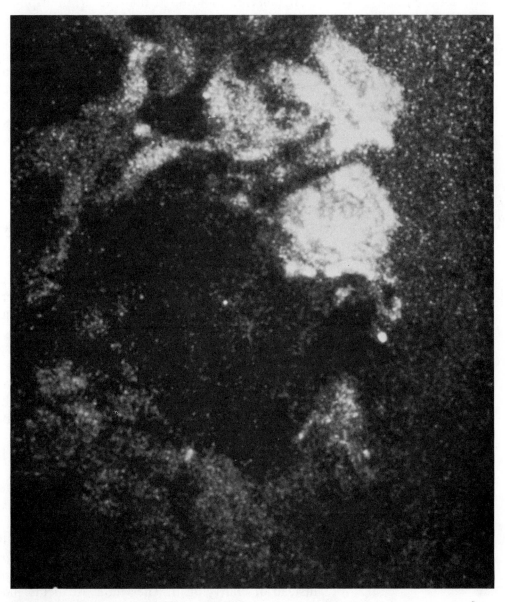

The famous "gargoyle head" shot taken by an AAS camera in June, 1975. The two protrusions on top seem like horns, a feature often mentioned by eyewitness accounts. Skeptics and believers alike were stunned by this photograph.

It must be mentioned that the original photographs were not clear. They had to be *computer enhanced* to show Nessie's features and body parts. Computer enhancement is a controversial technique, sometimes accused of distorting or changing an image. But it is accepted in many forms of research —especially astronomy—because it removes the "fog" which can cloud images on film. By doing so, it brings forth images which in the original picture were not seen. A computer does the work by sorting particles that make up a picture, separating the darker ones from the lighter ones, and making an image stand out more clearly.

After computer enhancement, the Nessie photographs were indeed very authentic looking, according to many experts. In addition, sonar echoes seemed to indicate something had been moving in the vicinity at the same time the photographs were taken. So convinced were they that the search had ended, members of the Academy of Applied Science planned a meeting with the distinguished scientists of the Royal Society of Edinburgh, the University of Edinburgh, and Heriot-Watt University. After that, the Nessie evidence would be brought before the British Parliament, which was already considering laws to protect the lake creature. The new proof from the Academy would be all that was needed to get the Nessie protection laws passed.

The problem seemed to be solved, or at least working toward a solution. Then newspapers heard about the originally unclear photos which showed a large creature or object only after being subjected to computer enhancement. The process is suspect by some because it may distort, or worsen a photograph instead of clarifying it. The whole Academy plan blew up in smoke. "Nessie, This Is Your Best Show Yet," read a *Sunday Times* of London headline. The press, among its other comments, suggested the photos might be a lost Viking ship, a diver with his mask on backward, or a fake movie monster lost in the loch.

There was so much publicity, so many letters to the editor, so many stories with wild claims, that the British scientists cancelled the historic meeting with the Academy. It was no longer possible, they said, to discuss the Nessie evidence without bias. And with all the publicity, no scientist was willing to risk losing a professional reputation if there were the remotest chance that the photos might ultimately prove to be a fake.

As a result, the Academy was able only to hold a brief meeting at the British Parliament in December 1975. They carefully placed before its members all the Nessie evidence. While the evidence looked good, it did not look good enough. Among the questions asked: Why were the Academy cameras able to take clear pictures of eel and salmon in the lake waters, but only unclear ones of the monster?

Is There Support From Science?

A few zoologists and paleontologists agreed there obviously were large creatures living in Loch Ness. For example, Dr. George Zug of Washington, D.C.'s Smithsonian Institution said he believed there were large creatures about twenty to thirty feet long living in the lake. The smaller items depicted on the sonar record might have been fish, Zug said, but the larger objects were "the recently described *Nessitera rhombopteryx* , previously known as the Loch Ness monsters." *Nessitera rhombopteryx* is a term combining the name of the Loch with the Greek word *teras*, meaning "marvel" or "strange creature." *Rhombopteryx* combines the Greek rhombos, a "diamond shape," with the Greek *pteryx*, meaning "fin" or "wing." Together, it translates as "the Ness monster with diamond-shaped fin."

Zug went on to comment about the pictures, saying, "This new evidence on the existence of a popu-

"I personally find the photographs extremely intriguing and sufficiently suggestive of a large aquatic animal to both urge and recommend that, in the future, more intensive investigations similar to the type pioneered in the past be undertaken in the loch."

Biologist A.W. Crompton quoted in *Is There A Loch Ness Monster?*

"We have no means of eliminating the possibility that a hoax has been perpetrated by a party unknown to the photographic team."

London's Natural History Museum senior zoology staff quoted in *Is There a Loch Ness Monster?*

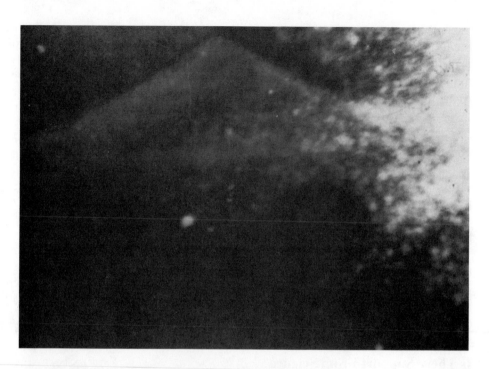

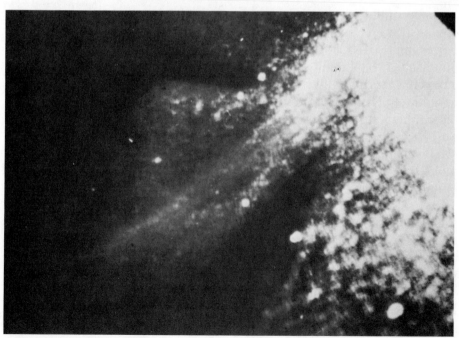

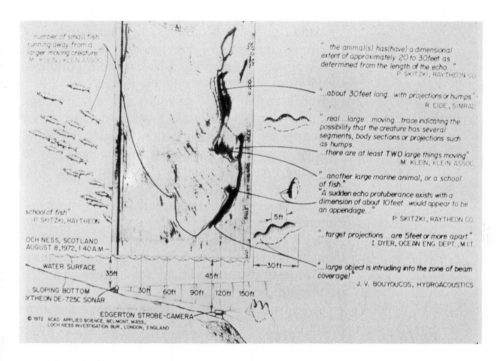

number of small fish
running away from a
larger moving creature."
M. KLEIN, KLEIN ASSOC.

"...the animal(s) has(have) a dimensional
extent of approximately 20 to 30 feet as
determined from the length of the echo..."
P. SKITZKI, RAYTHEON CO.

"...about 30 feet long...with projections or humps."
R. EIDE, SIMRAD

"...real...large...moving...trace indicating the
possibility that the creature has several
segments, body sections or projections such
as humps...
...there are at least TWO large things moving."
M. KLEIN, KLEIN ASSOC.

"...another large marine animal, or a school
of fish."
"A sudden echo protuberance exists with a
dimension of about 10 feet...would appear to be
an appendage..."
P. SKITZKI, RAYTHEON CO.

"...target projections...are 5 feet or more apart."
I. DYER, OCEAN ENG. DEPT., M.I.T.

"...large object is intruding into the zone of beam
coverage!"
J. V. BOUYOUCOS, HYDROACOUSTICS

school of fish"
P. SKITZKI, RAYTHEON

LOCH NESS, SCOTLAND
AUGUST 8, 1972, 1.40 A.M.

WATER SURFACE   35ft   45ft   30ft

SLOPING BOTTOM   30ft 60ft 90ft 120ft 150ft
RAYTHEON DE-725C SONAR

EDGERTON STROBE-CAMERA
© 1972 ACAD. APPLIED SCIENCE, BELMONT, MASS.,
LOCH NESS INVESTIGATION BUR., LONDON, ENGLAND

5ft

lation of large animals in Loch Ness should serve to encourage research on the natural history of Loch Ness and its plant and animal inhabitants, and remove the stigma of 'crackpot' from any scientist or group of scientists who wish to investigate the biological phenomena in Loch Ness."

Dr. Christopher McGowen, Associate Curator of the Department of Vertebrate Paleontology of Toronto's Royal Ontario Museum, also spoke out in favor of Nessie. "I am satisfied," he said, "that there is sufficient weight of evidence to support that there is an unexplained phenomenon of considerable interest in Loch Ness; the evidence suggests the presence of large aquatic animals."

Similar statements were made by other distinguished scientists, including Dr. A.W. Crompton of Harvard University, Sir Peter Scott, past chairman of the British National Appeal of the World Wildlife Fund, and David B. Stone, chairman of the New

The elapsed time photographs taken by AAS cameras of what appears to be a creature with flippers. A sonar tracking image of whatever tripped the cameras is shown above.

England Aquarium. Mr. Stone and other members of the Aquarium board of directors also suggested that the Academy act to protect Nessie from pollution, boat traffic, and other harmful conditions.

But, as usual, there were scientific dissenters. According to author Gerald Snyder, the five senior zoologists and paleontologists at London's Natural History Museum "seemed to go out of their way to state that the photographs did not prove the existence of large living animals in Loch Ness."

In summary, they stated there was no means of eliminating the possibility that someone was playing a joke on the Academy photographic team. They thought the photos were quite unclear, and any decision regarding them was merely guesswork. "It occurred to some of us," they mentioned, "that the head and neck photographs of the lake creature might be attributable to the presence of a large number of small gas bubbles such as are found in the air sacks of the phantom midges [a gnatlike insect] which are known to occur in large swarms." It sounded like these scientists were calling the Nessie pictures a series of bug photos.

Even more insulting, one English critic stated, "The picture just looks like a triangular piece of shortbread."

Continuing the Search

Far from being discouraged by this latest setback, the Academy moved forward in its search for proof. This time they were financially aided by *The New York Times*. With ample money, in 1976 the Academy was able to bring to the loch six underwater cameras—three 35 millimeter cameras, a 16 millimeter elapsed-time camera, a Polaroid SX-70, and a television camera. Every sixteen seconds, the elapsed-time camera automatically clicked. Every sixteen seconds, a 100-watt strobe light flashed to illuminate the elusive monster for the television monitors.

This 1976 expedition took 108,000 pictures. Those that showed anything at all, showed small fish or eels. The massive project, with all its people, noise, and lights perhaps scared the shy Nessie, for it did not even appear once.

Not that local residents minded. Business was booming, with Nessie posters everywhere. A Nessie picture-drawing contest was held for school children, and the winner got to pose with the Academy expedition crew. Runner-ups got binoculars for monster watching.

Attempts to lure the monster were many, and often extremely bizarre. A West German tourist

The Goodyear blimp Europa carried Loch Ness investigators over Urquhart Bay in June, 1982. The vessel in the bay was also part of this research effort.

sprinkled the lake's surface with ten tons of bread crumbs, hoping to lure Nessie up for a meal. Apparently Nessie was on a diet, for it did not even nibble. A British businessman tried hauling a piano around the lake, playing both Chopin and Bach classical pieces, hoping Nessie would come to shore. But music didn't tempt the beast.

Boats filled with eager tourists cruised Loch Ness, all waiting for a glimpse of the creature. Many were excited just to say they had been there. The cruise company even took out an insurance policy for the family of any person carried off by Nessie. Around the lake and in the city of Inverness, the community garbage cans bore the message, "Look for Nessie—but don't be messy!"

There were Nessie postcards, figurines, candy canes, postcards, T-shirts, pens, pencils, and pocket-knives. Nessie was not just a monster, it had become an entire industry. While all this made for nice profit, it hurt the scientific Nessie search. Every time a bit of new evidence was found, there was an immediate accusation about storeowners wanting to take in more money.

But the scientific hunt continued, spurred onward perhaps by being so close to the truth, yet not able to reach it. In 1979 the Academy of Applied Science planned a search using sonar-triggered cameras and strobe lights mounted on three trained dolphins. "Everything is falling into place," said Dr. Robert H. Rines in a *New York Times* article. According to Rines, the dolphins had no problem carrying the equipment. Using it, they were able to locate and photograph large underwater creatures such as sea turtles and sharks.

All was going well until one of the dolphins died and a replacement could not be trained in time for the project. "Plans for continuation of the project have been postponed but at this time have not been cancelled," said Howard Curtis, executive vice president of the Academy of Applied Science.

In 1980, Nessie's Russian cousin, supposedly living in Lake Kok-Kol in Kazakhstan was proved to be an Ice Age moraine filling a deep crater. A moraine is an accumulation of stones, rocks, gravel and other debris carried and deposited by a glacier. According to the *London Times*, water intake into the crater's channels causes small whirlpools. This makes the surface of Kok-Kol "show a snake-like motion resembling the body of a deep water monster."

In 1983, *The Wall Street Journal* reported that Avril Deacon, Caron McNichol and Jimmy Nairn of the Highlands area were driving along the highway near the loch when they saw a "dark shape" in the water. The dark shape soon rose to the surface and began swimming. "I have never seen anything like it in my life," said McNichol. Too bad nobody had a camera.

Sylvester

The same year, a retired Scottish electronics engineer, Robert P. Craig, stated in *New Scientist* magazine that Nessie was really "Sylvester," his name for an ancient Scotch pine tree.

In an explanation widely covered in newspapers as prestigious as *The Wall Street Journal*, Craig said that Sylvester fell into the lake many years ago. Gases formed in its trunk. These gases drove resin and tar oils toward the stumps of the tree's branches. That caused blisters filled with tiny gas bubbles to form. The blisters acted like tiny elevating balloons filled with gas, so Sylvester began rising to the surface. Then, one day, perhaps when one of the monster watchers was watching, the ancient Scotch pine popped out of the water—and there was another Nessie report.

This sounded like a plausible explanation. There was only one slight mistake. As monster-hunter Ronald Binns pointed out, "Loch Ness is not now,

Operation Deep Scan, conducted in October 1987. The boats were equipped with sonar scanning equipment, and they swept the loch from shore to shore to try and pick up Nessie's movements. The results were negative.

Adrian Shine, director of Operation Deep Scan.

and never has been, a place surrounded by Scotch pines."

The dispute made for good media coverage, but didn't solve the Nessie problem. Did it or did it not exist in Loch Ness?

The Search Today

By 1984, Tim Dinsdale had spent twenty-five years searching for the hide-and-seek creature, visiting Loch Ness fifty times. While he took many photos, some seeming to show a moving creature, no photo has ever been clear enough to satisfy scientists.

By the end of 1985, the only really strange creature seen at the lake was a seal. However Nessie searchers did find a bomber at 230 feet down that had crashed at the beginning of World War II.

But the monster-hunters were and are unstop-

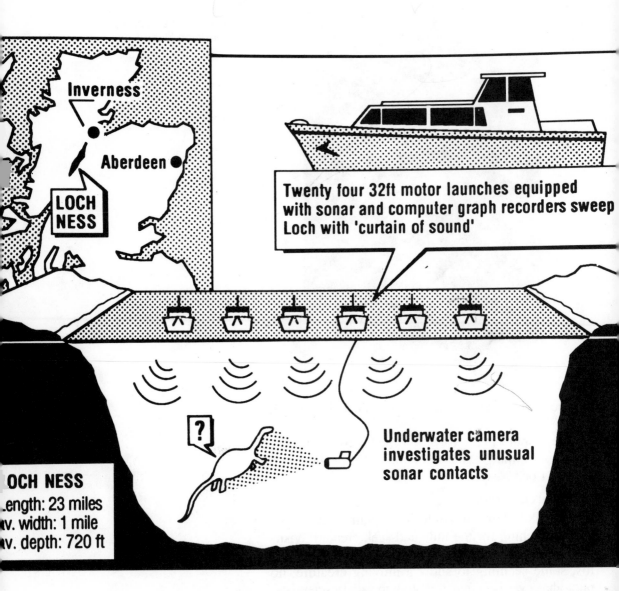

Operation Deep Scan used sonar to penetrate the loch and create an underwater picture with sound from shore to shore.

pable. The Official Loch Ness Monster Exhibition took place in 1987. As part of this, about thirty boats participated in a $1.6 million project called "Operation Deep Scan," led by naturalist Adrian Shine. These boats spent a month checking over the entire lake with sonar. "If we can send men to the moon," stated Anthony Harmsworth, curator of the exhibition, "surely we can discover whether or not the Loch Ness Monster exists."

Something did show up on the sonar record, moving about 600 feet down. "No one here was prepared to say that it was the Loch Ness Monster," a *Washington Post* reporter said, "but few would swear it wasn't."

In the meantime, over 200,000 tourists visited the exhibition display of Nessie photographs, fiberglass models, and filmstrips. Nessie, however, did not make a personal appearance.

Perhaps it was in the lake. And perhaps it was not. "The sure way to drive these reticent creatures into extinction," said a *New York Times* article, "is to mount elaborate search expeditions."

Is it possible that Nessie was truly in the lake once, and all the hullaballoo drove it away, or worse?

"The machine hasn't been invented yet that will let us know," said author Tim Cole in *Science* magazine.

But perhaps someone will invent it tomorrow.

Conclusion

The Evidence Is Inconclusive

Opposite page: the Loch Ness monster, photographed from Urquhart Castle by Anthony Shiels on May 21, 1977.

There often seems to be an attitude among biologists that if something cannot be cut up in a laboratory, it does not exist. "I think you really prove the crime when you've got the corpse," said said one determined Nessie opponent on a 1961 BBC radio show.

Yet unlike most tales of weird beasts, many of the estimated 10,000 Loch Ness sightings reported have been made by apparently sensible people who have nothing to gain by speaking out about a monster: doctors, farmers, housewives, teachers, police officers, and retired Highland residents who dislike the crowds Nessie brings in.

There may have been many thousand more sightings which have not been reported for fear of ridicule. "I'll never say I saw it," is the attitude of hundreds of witnesses to strange physical objects, including water monsters, according to authors Janet and Colin Bord in their book *Alien Animals*

Once gossip got out in Inverness that an elderly museum curator had seen Nessie. This man had always scoffed at the monster's existence. When reporters finally cornered him about the rumor, the

> "Everybody knows there's something in the loch. The question is what are these big things we seem to be tracking with sonar and are getting underwater pictures of?"
>
> Attorney Robert Rines, quoted in *Is There A Loch Ness Monster?*

> "Ladbrokes, the bookmakers, yesterday opened a book on the Loch Ness monster. They are offering odds of 33 to 1 against its existence being proved."
>
> Article in the *London Times*

curator was asked if what he had seen looked like the descriptions of Nessie. The man reddened and gasped out, "Aye, and I'll say noo moore about it."

In general, Nessie reputedly has a small snake-like head, long slim neck, heavy body, long powerful tail, one to three humps, and four diamond-shaped fins or flippers. It is brownish-gray and between fifteen and fifty feet long. The more unusual descriptions include those mentioning up to fifteen humps, horse's mane, forked tail, wispy beard, mouth full of sharp teeth, fangs, a dragon's head, snail-like stalk on top of its head, stumpy horns, and occasional moans like a foghorn.

Scientists say that despite the multiple sightings, no physical evidence of unusual lake creatures has ever been found: corpses, fossils, skeletons, samples of hair or skin, footprints, or any other remnant.

On the other hand, there are photographs which, together with eyewitness reports, suggest to many people that Nessie is occasionally visible. At least something that markedly resembles a monster can be seen. But there is no absolute proof of Nessie's existence. Is this because no creature exists, or, is it as author F.W. Holiday says: "The phenomenon seems purposefully to evade the photographer, or photographs do not develop, or mysteriously vanish, or the camera was left in the car."

A strange ill luck does seem to haunt the Loch Ness monster hunters. There can be a fully staffed observation post, but Nessie waits until the persons are otherwise occupied to appear. For example, in 1965 watchers reported that the monster showed itself on the one day the Loch Ness Investigation Bureau's camera was out of order. In 1970, it appeared minutes after the observer had packed up for the evening. In 1971, author Tim Dinsdale missed the shot he had waited years for when Nessie appeared only two hundred yards away from him. Paralyzed with shock at his dreams coming true, he

The entire frame of the Surgeon's Photograph.
Will Nessie ever present itself in a clear, verifiable photograph?

did not take the photo.

Doc Shiels of Cornwall, who took a series of color photographs in 1977, reports: "My original No. 1 color slide went astray for days on end at the *Daily Record* newspaper in Glasgow. Other photographs from the same film vanished entirely after being inspected by the picture editor. My original No. 2 slide somehow escaped from its carefully sealed envelope while in the mail. It's a disturbing fact that hardly any of the original negatives of the better known Loch Ness monster photographs taken since 1933 have survived. Nessie pix are supernaturally accident-prone!"

Will We Ever Know?

Monster hunters, and monster-hunting organizations, have come and gone from the lake area. They have tried almost everything to find Nessie. They have set up cameras around the lake and taken thousands of hours of film. They have cruised the lake silently in a sailboat so they would not disturb the creature. They have sent submarines down into the lake's dark depths. They have even tried tempting Nessie with bait—both music and food. But no technique has worked.

Skeptics call Nessie a rotting log, frolicking otter, canoe, floating oil barrel, roe deer, boat ripple, vegetation mats, telephone pole, waves, ducks, unusual lighting effects, a cormorant, gas bubbles, giant squid, mirage, giant eel, salmon, stickleback, char, pike, large sturgeon, whale, shark, sea cow, water current, turtle, crocodile, and elephant.

Others remark that a great deal of business has come to Loch Ness along with its monster, and perhaps the business came first. "One cannot deny," author Henry Bauer writes, "that the souvenir shops sell models of Nessies in cloth, clay, and plastic, and Nessie T-shirts, emblems, and guide books. But that is small potatoes; a determined effort to make money

Keeping watch on Loch Ness.

from the presence of Nessie would surely involve hotels and campgrounds overlooking the loch, viewing platforms with coin-operated binoculars, and constructing boat marinas—the things that are simply not to be found around Loch Ness."

Because the matter of the "Nessies" is widely regarded as "pseudoscience" or false science, at best, it is hard to get information printed in scientific journals. "Although the critics so often cry 'no scientific evidence,'" authors Janet and Colin Bord relate, "when it is provided they are equally able to ignore it."

Author Philip Stalker, writing about the Loch Ness monster in 1957, commented that "if medical science had shown as little enterprise and as little

Will science ever prove that Nessie, the mysterious serpent, lives in Loch Ness? Only a captured specimen will solve the mystery for good.

courage in its various fields, as marine zoologists have shown in regard to the Loch Ness animal, appendicitis would still be a fatal illness and tuberculosis would be killing millions every year in Britain."

The result of scientific indifference or fear is often poorly reproduced photographs and undigested hearsay printed mainly in newspapers and magazines that seek out the sensational. This helps to give the doubtful the impression that the monster is science fiction. It also contributes to the problem author Bauer refers to as the "incomplete and fragmented publication of the data from Loch Ness...What has long been needed and is still lacking is the publication of results as they are obtained, with strict editorial control to ensure that all the relevant details are described, loopholes in reasoning plugged, gaps in data filled in or at least acknowledged."

Bauer agrees there is no truly conclusive and direct evidence to work with. But "the capture of a live specimen or the recovery of a carcass or skeleton, after all, would settle the matter. A substantial reason for disbelief, then, lies in the fact that the best case for Nessie at this stage remains a circumstantial one. And circumstantial cases leave room for doubt."

Yet "more and more individuals, groups, and scientific people," engineer Tim Dinsdale writes, "are lending their support and equipment in an attempt to solve the mystery, which genuinely remains one of the greatest unsolved mysteries on earth."

"It would be a sad comment on human beings if a creature which had come down unchanged and unharmed from prehistory was to be finally exterminated by modern man."

Biologist Gerald Durrell, quoted in *The Loch Ness Story*

"Nessie may end up at Disneyland—performing twice a day, catching frozen fish in her mouth on cue."

Journalist Eric Sevareid, quoted in *Is There a Loch Ness Monster?*

Glossary

Aquatic living in water

Biologist person who studies the life of animals and plants

Computer Enhancement a controversial technique used to remove any fogging which clouds photographic images on film. Some say it distorts or changes the image.
Controversy a dispute or debate
Curator the director of a museum

Exhibition a collection of objects put on display
Extinct no longer in existence; having died out

Flipper a wide, flat limb adapted for swimming

Mammal an animal which nurses its babies, has hair, and gives birth to live young
Marine Zoologist a zoologist who studies the sea

Nessitera Rhombopteryx a scientific term combining the name of the Loch with the Greek word *teras*, meaning "marvel" or "strange creature." *Rhombopteryx* combines the Greek word *rhombos*, a "diamond shape," with *pteryx*, meaning "fin" or "wing." Together, it translates as "the Ness monster with diamond-shaped fin."

Paleontologist a scientist who studies fossils

Reptile air-breathing, cold blooded vertebrates
(such as snakes)

Sonar a device for detecting underwater objects
and fishusing sound waves; the echoes they send
back when they strike an underwater object can
locate the object

Strobe Light an electron tube which produces brief,
high intensity light flashes

Theory an arrangement of facts explaining a real or
assumed phenomenon

Zoology the science which studies the natural history of animals, their habits, and their body
mechanisms

For Further Exploration

Janet & Colin Bord, *Alien Animals*. Pennsylvania: Stackpole Books, 1981.

John Godwin, *This Baffling World*. New York: Hart Publishing, 1968.

Patricia Lauber, *Mystery Monsters of Loch Ness*. Illinois: Garrard Publishing, 1978.

Gerald Snyder, *Is There A Loch Ness Monster?* New York: Julian Messner, 1978.

James B. Sweeney. *Sea Monster*. New York: David McKay Company, 1977.

Ian Thorne, *The Loch Ness Monster*. Minnesota: Crestwood House, 1979.

Additional Bibliography

Henry H. Bauer, *The Enigma of Loch Ness*.
   Chicago: University of Illinois Press, 1988.

Tim Dinsdale, *Loch Ness Monster*. London:
   Routledge & Kegan Paul, 1966.

Tim Dinsdale, *Project Water Horse*. London:
   Routledge & Kegan Paul, 1975.

Dennis Meredith, *Search at Loch Ness*. New York:
   The New York Times Book Company, 1977.

Nicholas Witchell, *The Loch Ness Story*. Maryland:
   Penguin Books, 1975.

Index

Picture Credits

About the Author

Robert D. San Souci is the author of the award-winning *The Legend of Scarface* (a *New York Times* Best Illustrated Children's Book of the Year 1978 and a Children's Book Council Notable Children's Trade Book in the Field of Social Studies in 1978), *The Song of Sedna* (a Children's Book Council Notable Children's Trade Book in the Field of Social Studies in 1981), *Casey's Color Surprise* (a book/cassette combination for Playskool/Hasbro) and *The Brave Little Tailor*.

Other published works for juveniles include *The Legend of Sleepy Hollow* (1986) and *The Enchanted Tapestry* (1987), each named a Children's Book Council Notable Children's Trade Book in the Field of Social Studies, as well as *Short and Shivery*, honored as a Children's Choice Book for 1987.

The author, a native Californian and graduate of St. Mary's College in Moraga, was formerly employed by Harper & Row, Publishers, San Francisco, in the marketing and editorial departments, and now works full time at his writing. He has taught numerous classes throughout Northern California on writing books for children and adults; is frequently invited to speak to school classes and parents' groups; and has lectured at San Francisco State University, California State University at Fresno, and for the American Library Association. He lives in the San Francisco Bay Area.